Edited by Maylene Dence and Phyllis Klein

Book Design by Taji Parks

Free Advent Banner Publishing

LESSONS in the Old Testament
FOR SENIOR CLASSES.

LESSON 1
April 7, 2018

THE WAY OF THE RIGHTEOUS

Ps 1:1-6
(MEMORY VERSES Ps 1:1-6.)

GOLDEN TEXT " Blessed is the man that walketh not in the counsel or the ungodly, nor standeth in the way of sinners, nor sitteth in the seat of the scornful." Ps 1:1

1. With what does the book of Psalms open ? Ps 1:1, first word

NOTE.—The first psalm has no title in the original, as have most of the others. It was, doubtless, written by David. It opens, as does also the book, with a benediction. The word translated " blessed " is in the plural, denoting "blessednesses," and, according to some scholars, could well be translated, " Oh, the blessednesses [or happinesses] of the man! " etc., including all blessings of God's grace. It is well to notice that this blessing is based solely on character.

2. Upon whom is such blessing pronounced? Ps 1:1

3. What is the first step generally taken in wickedness? Ps 1:1, first clause

> NOTE—Walking, in "the counsel of the ungodly," imitating their ways, seeking their advice and help, are generally the first steps in backsliding from God. But the man who is blessed of God does not " walk " in the counsel of the ungodly; his counsel comes from God. See 2 Tim. 2: 22

4. What would naturally follow to him who walked in the counsel of the ungodly? Ps. 1:1, second clause.

NOTE—From heeding the counsel of the ungodly, from occasionally following their advice, a person comes at last to stand in the way of sinners. He deliberately chooses the "trodden path" of those who transgress God's law.

5. What would be the third stage of sin? Ps.1:1, third clause.

> NOTE—The man who departs from God at first walks in the counsel of the ungodly, those who know not God, till he deliberately chooses to stand, or, as given by some, "to tread" in the way (the "trodden path") of sinners, till at last the heart becomes hardened, and he takes his seat among those who openly deride and scoff at that which is good and pure and true; he chooses the assembly of mockers as his companions.

6. What leads to this hardness of heart? Heb., 3:13

7. With whom alone does the counsel of life rest? Isa. 11:1, 2

8. What is the character of the counsels of God? Isa. 25:1; Isa. 28:29

9. What will be the end of those who despise the counsel of God? Prov 1:29-32

10. What does the Psalmist say of the ungodly? Ps 1:4   *They are easily changed*

11. What are we assured of those who put their dependence in such? Jer 17:5, 6

12. What is said of their final end Ps 1:5, last clause of verse 6   *They will perish. They will not stand in the Judgement*

13. Who only will stand in the judgment? Ps 24:3, 4
Only those who have formed a right character

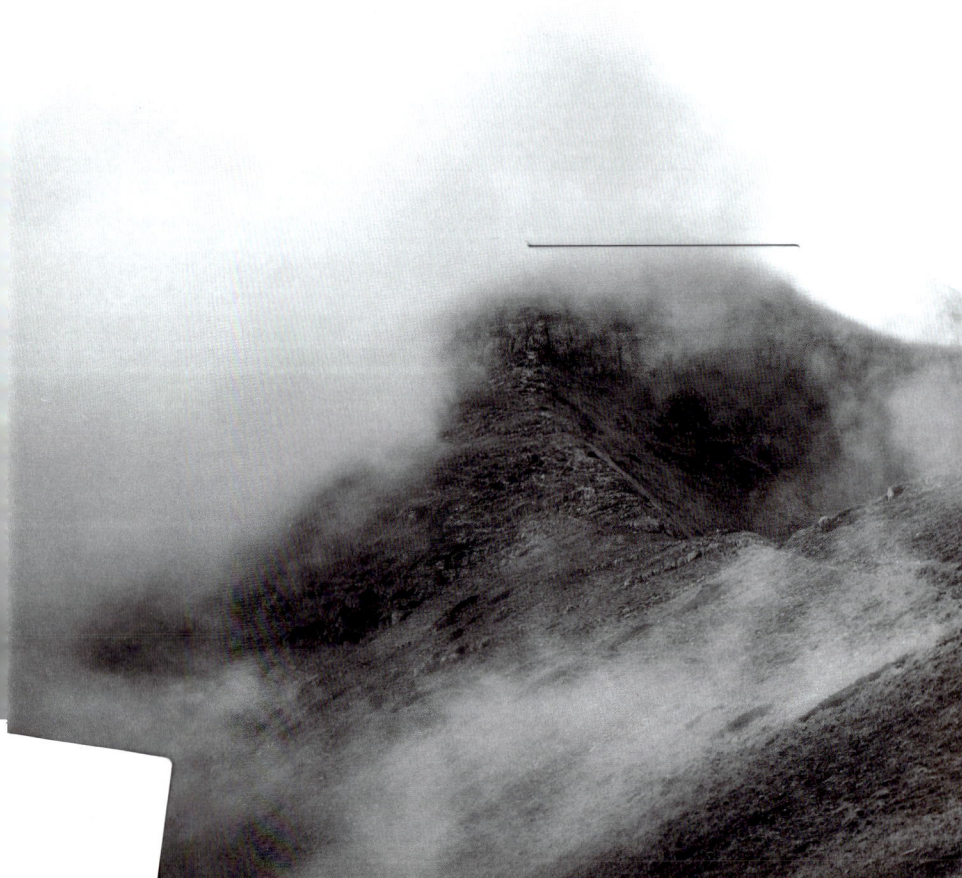

14. Through whom alone is such a character attained? I Cor 1:30; John 5:24

Christ

15. What change takes place in the heart of a man thus blessed? Eze 36:26

A new heart of flesh

16. How will he regard God's law? Eze. 36:27; Ps 1:2, Jer 31:33

17. To what is the Christian growth of such a man likened? Ps 1:3; Jer. 17:7, 8

18. What promise does God give to those who have sinned against him if they will but put away their sins and seek him with the whole heart? Isa 58:8, 11

19. What does he say of his prosperity? Ps 1:3, last clause

20. In what way do we "prosper" when we suffer persecution or peril? How do I come to know that all things work together for my good? Rom 8:35-37, 28
REWORDED—MD

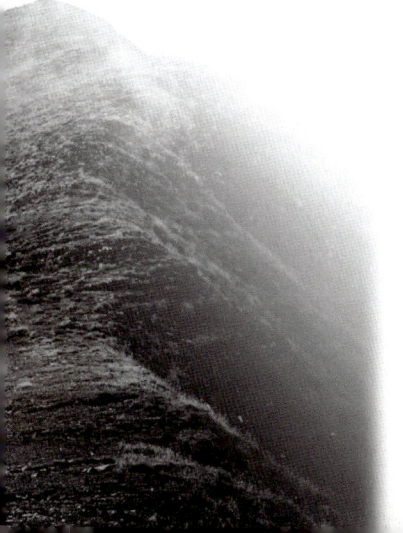

**LESSON 2
April 14, 2018
THE KING IN ZION**
Ps 2:1-12.
(MEMORY VERSES Ps 2:10-12)

GOLDEN TEXT " Blessed are all they that put their trust in Him." Ps 2:12.

NOTE.—The psalm under consideration is divided into four parts, as follows:
1. A prediction of the rejection of the Christ by the rulers of the world, when He came as the Anointed of God, and the result of their rejection.
2. The address of the Father to the nations.
3. The address of the Son.
4. An appeal of love and warning to the people.

THE PREDICTION.
1. What is said of the nations at the first advent of Christ? Ps 2:1

2. What did they do against Christ? Ps 2:2, 3

NOTE.—" Messiah", in Hebrew, and "Christ," in Greek, mean "anointed." See John 1: 41, margin. The Anointed of Jehovah is Christ the Lord. That anointing took place when he was manifested to the world as the Messiah. It was effected at his baptism, when the Holy Spirit, like a dove, rested upon him. John 1:32, 33; Acts 10:38

at would their counsel against God prove to be?
last clause.

4. What did their counsel really result in?
Acts 4:25-28; Rev 12:10

5. What great truth is this a confirmation of?
2 Cor 13:8

THE ADDRESS OF THE FATHER.

6. How did God regard their rage? Ps 2:4

7. Because of their thus rejecting God what will he do? Ps 2:5

8. When and by whom will this wrath finally be executed? 2 Thess 1:7-9

9. What has God done for His Son whom the people thought to destroy? Ps 2:6

10. Where is this hill of Zion? Heb 12:22

11. What position does Christ occupy there? Heb 8:1; Zech 6:13

THE ADDRESS OF THE SON.

12. What does Christ say he will declare? Ps 2:7, first part

13. What is this decree of God? Ps 2:7, last part

14. What time does this refer to? Acts 13:33; Heb 5:5

15. What did the resurrection show Jesus to be? Rom 1:3, 4

16. What assurance does God give him? Ps 2:8

17. What promise and oath of God will then be fulfilled? Gen 22:16-18

18. At what time will this be fulfilled? 1 Cor 15: 24-28

NOTE.—That the student may not be misled, we give the following paraphrase of 1 Cor 15: 24-28: "Then cometh the end [of Christ's reign on his Father's throne as priest, Zech 6: 12, 13; Rev. 3:21], when he [the Son] shall have delivered up the kingdom to God, even the Father ; when he [the Father] shall have put down all rule and all authority and power. For he [the Son] must reign [as priest], till he [the Father] hath put all enemies under his [the Son's] feet [as the Father promised in Ps 110:1]. The last enemy that shall be destroyed is death. For he [the Father] hath [in purpose, Eph 1:22,23] put all things under his [the Son's] feet. But when he [the Father] saith all things are put under him [the Son], it is manifest that he [the Father] is excepted, that did put all things under him [the Son]. And when all things shall be subdued unto him [the Son], then shall the Son also himself be subject unto him [the Father] that put all things under him [the Son], that God may be all in all." Then Christ takes his own throne. Matt 25: 31; Rev 3: 21

19. What will he do to those nations who at that time know him not? Ps 2:9; Matt 13: 39-42

THE LOVING APPEAL.

20. Before that great day of wrath comes, what appeal does God in mercy make through the gospel? Ps 2:10, 11

21. Instead of meditating evil against the Son, what does he entreat them to do? Ps 2:12

> NOTE. —The word translated "kiss" is evidently used in the sense of receiving, embracing, accepting. Some ancient authorities render, "Lay hold of (or receive) instruction," others, "Worship in purity." See margin of Revised Version.

22. At what time do we have assurance of salvation? 2 Cor 6:2; Heb 3:13; Gal 5:1, first clause

23. What gracious assurance does God give to all? John 6:37; Ps 2:12

LESSON 3
April 21, 2018
GOD'S WORKS AND WORD
PSALMS 19
(MEMORY VERSES Ps. 19:7-11)

GOLDEN TEXT. The law of the Lord is perfect, converting the soul. Ps. 19:7

NOTE- In this psalm are described two great manifestations of God, namely, his works and his word.

GOD IN HIS WORKS.
1. In what does the Psalmist say are the manifestations of God? Ps. 19:1

2. How frequently are God's glory and handiwork thus manifested? Ps. 19:2

3. How far-reaching is this instruction? Ps. 19:3, 4; Rom. 10:18

4. What responsibility does this revelation place upon man? Rom. 1:19, 20

NOTE.—It has been well said that the manifestation of God in the works of nature is his great primary school, day, school and night school.

5. How may it be said that man is left without excuse by the revelation which God makes of himself in his works?

NOTE.—God's works—the glory and beauty of the heavens and the earth proclaim a Being of infinite power, knowledge, wisdom, and glory. But a Being who is infinite in power and wisdom and knowledge must be infinite also in justice and mercy (or love, the combination of all goodness) so that a reflective soul desiring to know more of God would be led "from nature up to nature's God."

6. How does the Psalmist describe the most glorious of God's work manifest to us ? Ps 19:4-6

7. What is the sun a representation of?
Ans.—Of light and heat, a symbol of the light and life from God, warming, blessing all. Reworded MD

GOD IN HIS WORD OR LAW.
8. What reflects the character of a government?
Ans.—The law, for it is the kind of laws and their enforcement which make a government what it is.

9. What is said of the law of the Lord? Ps 19 :7, first clause

10. Can that which is perfect be made better or corrected?   Reworded MD

11. What is the effect of the law on the soul?
Ps 19: 7, first part

NOTE.—The law restores the soul by revealing the right way, pointing out its sin (1 John 3:4; .Rom 7:7) and need of a Saviour, and so leads to conversion. See Gal 3:22, 23

12. What is a second characteristic of God's law?
Ps 19: 7, last part

NOTE.—" Testimony" means witness. God's law is the witness of his character, and also witnesses to the righteousness of Christ in us. Rom 3:21 This (as well as all other kindred terms used in this connection) refers to the Decalogue. See Ex 25:16

13. What effect does the witness of God have upon the simple? Ps 19:7, last part; Ps 119:98-100

NOTE.—This witness is "sure;" it will never fail; it can be depended upon forever. "Amen" is derived from the same word. It makes wise the simple but ignorant, (not the foolish), who desire to know.

14. What third characteristic of God's law is mentioned and what is the result of embracing it? Ps 19:8, first part; Ps 119:111, 128

NOTE.—" Statutes " (Revised Version "precepts"), appointments, charges, which God has given. They are right and right alone, and hence the converted heart rejoices that it has found the right way.

15. What is the fourth characteristic of God's law and what is its effect? Ps. 19:8, last part; Ps 12:6

16. What is the fifth characteristic of that law and its effect? Ps 19:9, first part

NOTE.—" Fear," (that which demands reverence) is applied to the great and holy law of God's love, which demands on the part of the soul that reverence for God which is the beginning of wisdom. See Job 28:28; Prov 1:7; Prov 8:13. God's law endures forever. Ps 19:9

17. What sixth characteristic and its effect are noted? Ps 19:9, last part; 119:160

18. What effect do all these qualities have upon the converted soul? Ps 19:10

> NOTE—The testimony of this psalm to the law of God is the universal testimony of the entire Bible. The law of God, like its Author, is perfect, sure, right, clean, true, and righteous altogether, and, says Paul, holy, just, good, spiritual. Rom 7: 12, 14. There is only one reason why we should hate God's law, and that is the possession of the carnal mind. Rom 8:7

19. By what means and by whom may we be brought to love God's law? Rom 1:16, 17; Eze 36:26, 27

20. What question does the Psalmist ask and what petition does he offer? Ps 19: 12

> NOTE.—Secret faults, faults not seen or realized by Himself (or maybe faults he's trying to hide from others?).
> last comment by MD

21. Who only knows the heart? By what agency does God reveal it to us? Jer 17:9, 10; Ps 19:11, first part; Rom. 7:7.

22. From what sins does David earnestly pray to be kept? Ps 19:13

> NOTE.—Presumptuous sins seem to be set opposite the secret faults, or, rather, secret faults and presumptuous sins make up the sum total of all sin. Presumptuous sins are sins committed knowing them to be wrong, presuming

on God's mercy, or thinking that God is not particular. They may exist in all degrees, from slight departures from God to the utmost defiance, as was the case in Num 15: 30, 31. See also, Lev 10:1, 2; 2 Sam 6:3-7

We may commit secret faults without a violation of conscience, because we do not know we have them, although others may. But we cannot commit known sins without presuming on God's mercy and benumbing our conscience; and in stupefying conscience we fall rapidly till we commit much transgression. Let us continually pray that such sins may not have dominion over us. One of the most blessed of friends is a conscience made and kept tender by the Spirit of God.

23. What, on the other hand, is said of keeping God's commandments? Ps 19:11; Rev 22:14.

NOTE.—There is not only a reward FOR keeping God's commandments, as is implied in the last scripture, but there is a reward in keeping them, in doing God's will by the grace of Christ, and in walking with him.

24. What should be the daily prayer of every heart? Ps 19:14.

LESSON 4
April 28, 2018
THE LORD MY SHEPHERD
PSALM 23
(MEMORY VERSES Ps 23:1-6.)

GOLDEN TEXT " The Lord is my shepherd; I shall not want." Ps 23:1.

1. Who does David say is his shepherd? Ps 23:1, first part. The word "Lord" comes from "Jehovah."

2. Through whom was Jehovah especially manifested in such a tender relation? John 10:11, first clause, Heb 13:20

NOTE—It has been well remarked that if we would appreciate the infinite trust and tenderness expressed in this psalm, we must take into consideration the life of the Syrian shepherd. He was constantly with his sheep, nearly always alone. However large his flock, he knew every sheep by name, and every sheep knew him. In the cool, frosty nights, in the fierce heat of the noonday sun, in the storm and tempest, in the rocky, rugged way as well as in the green pastures, he was identified with his flock, leading them to pastures of plenty, or imperiling his life for their safety. All this was known to David, to Moses, to Jacob, and others. I Sam 17:34-36; Ex 3:1; Gen 31:38-40

3. What assurance may we draw from the fact that the Lord is our Shepherd? Ps 23:1, last clause

17

4. What basis have we for such assurance?
Col 1:19, Col 2:9

5. What does Jesus say of the relation between him and his people? John 10:14, 15

NOTE—The Revised Version reads thus: " I am the Good Shepherd; and I know mine own, and mine own know me, even as the Father knoweth me, and I know the Father." They are all united by the same bond of union, namely, the "life that is in God."

6. How great is the love which Christ bears for his sheep.
John 10:15, last clause

7. Is such love manifested only toward the faithful? Isa 53:5, 6

8. What contrast does he draw between the true and false shepherds? John 10:11-13

9. How do his sheep regard his voice?
Ps 23:2-4, John 10:2-4

10. How do the sheep of the Lord regard the voice of strangers? John 10:5

11. What blessing does he bestow upon them? Ps 23:2

NOTE.—The life of the Christian is not all conflict. God gives the precious privilege now and then of quiet, refreshing resting-places, where the soul may feed on the bread of life, and rest while it partakes; where the longing heart may wander beside "the waters of rest," the waters which bring rest, the communion of the Spirit of God. Thus it is that we are prepared for the conflict, as such quiet and abundant feeding restores the lean and fainting sheep, and fits them for enduring long and tiresome journeys.

12. What is the effect of these restful blessings of God? Ps 23:3, first part.

13. How is the soul kept in this condition? Ps 23:3.

14. For whose sake does God grant all these blessings to his people? Same verse.

NOTE.—This is a thought which should be ever kept before us. God grants us no blessings because of our worth to him. It is wholly by his grace, wholly for his name's sake. It is often pity for the lost sheep which moves the true shepherd to go forth, frequently imperiling his life for its rescue. It was unmerited pity and boundless love alone which moved the heart of the Great Shepherd to give his life for the sheep.

15. How fully may we expect the Shepherd's presence in the journey of life? Ps 23:4, first part. The expression, "valley of the shadow of death" denotes the profoundest darkness, but Christ will be with us, even in our greatest trial.

16. What comfort does the Christian have in this darkness? Ps 23. 4; Isa 50:10.

NOTE.—" Rod " is used to denote a kingly scepter, a symbol of power, an instrument of correction and guidance. It would fitly symbolize God's law, which, like the shepherd's crook, brings the straying back to the path of safety. See our last lesson. " Staff" denotes a stay or support," a means of defense, and would fittingly represent the gospel, the aggregation of all God's promises, the only hope and stay of the people of God. In Zech 11: 7 the shepherd had two staves; the name of one was " Beauty" (margin, " Graciousness"); the name of the other. was " Bands " (margin, " Binders " or " Union").

See Revised Version. These would fittingly represent in the Great Shepherd the gospel and law, the fullness of God's word, but, unlike the earthly shepherd's staves, they can never be broken. "Comfort" does not simply mean to console, but to strengthen and establish. And that soul who trusts in the gospel of Christ, whose feet are set in the way of his commandments, is indeed comforted and established.

17. What triumph does God give his servant in the midst of his enemies? Ps 23:5, Rom 8:35, 37

18. What is always the result of one's cup running over with God's blessings? Ps 40:3

19. From the Psalmist's confidence in God, what does he conclude? Ps 23:6

NOTE—The word "follow" means that His goodness and mercy will "hunt me down" all the days of my life.
 Note by MD

20. In what house of God did the Psalmist expect to dwell? Eph 2:19-22

LESSON 5
May 5, 2018
THE PRAYER OF THE PENITENT
PS 51:1-13.
(MEMORY VERSES, Ps 51:10-13.)

GOLDEN TEXT " Create in me a clean heart, 0 God; and renew a right [constant) spirit within me." Ps 51:10

INTRODUCTION The title to this psalm doubtless gives its origin, but it is adapted to sinners of every age and clime. It expresses the condition of a soul truly humble and penitent.

1. On what basis does David plead God's mercy? Ps 51:1, first part

2. Through what alone may we obtain pardon? Titus 3:5-7

3. On what ground did David plead that the record of his sin might be blotted out or wiped away? Ps 51:1, last part

NOTE—Mark the gradations, " mercy," "loving-kindness," "multitude of God's tender mercies." Have compassion, pity, tenderness toward me, not in stinted measure, for my sin is great, but according to thy lovingkindness, even to blot out my transgressions (which are many) " according to the multitude of thy tender mercies." The sinner's large plea for God's undeserved mercy. shows a large conception of his sin.

4. Does the truly penitent wish to retain any of his sin? Ps 51:2

NOTE—Some versions have "t-h-o-r-o-u-g-h-l-y," while the English versions have "t-h-r-o-u-g-h-l-y." They both mean the same. The latter is the older form. The word means "through and through."

5. On what condition does God forgive sin? 1 John 1:9

6. Did David meet these conditions? Ps 51:3

7. How did he regard his sin in relation to God? Ps 51:4, first part

NOTE—It is said that the Hebrew manner of expression includes and swallows up all lesser things in the greater, so that David's sin against God was so great that it shut the other sins from his sight, so to speak. Another way of looking at the text is this: David as king could be called to account by no one save God, hence his sin was against God as his sovereign. But in whatever way the Psalmist used the expression as regards the particular wrongs done to Uriah the Hittite, the only true sorrow for sin is that when the sinner considers the greatest sin of all as committed against God.

8. What acknowledgment does he make as to God's justice? Ps 51:4

9. By what does he show that he recognizes the root of his sin? Ps 51:5

NOTE.—He who fails to realize that mortal flesh is essentially depraved, and that only the power of God within can overcome the weaknesses and passions of the flesh, will be defeated by the enemy. See Rom 7:14-24; Rom 8:2,3   David recognized, as every sinner should, not only the enormity of his particular sin, but the inherent depravity of the natural man. There is no reflection against his parents; the words are true of every soul of man.

10. How does God desire truth to affect man ? Ps 51:6; 15:2

11. What would the possession of this inner truth and wisdom do for David? Prov 3:13; Ps 51:6

12. How does David continue to plead with God in regard to sin ? Ps 51:7, 8

NOTE—It will be seen by reference to Lev 14:3-7 that the purging of hyssop was not merely the cleansing. It was an authoritative acquittal, or pronouncement that the man was clean. David desires to be made perfectly clean; he wants God's complete acquittal. He desires to rejoice in the sentence of acquittal. His spiritual fall he likens to a physical fall in which the bones have been broken; he wants perfect healing from his fall.

13 . How does he plead that God will regard his sins ? Ps 51:9

14. What alone can hide our sins from God? Rom 3:22; Rom 4:6, 7

15. Is it simply forgiveness alone that the truly penitent desires? Ps 51:10, margin

16. By what power are the new heart and spirit given? 2 Cor 5:17, 18; Eze 36:26

17. Whose spirit is then within us and how does it affect us? Rom 8:9; Eze 36:27

18. Whose companionship does the truly repentant long for? Ps 51:11

19. What great boon does he ask of God? Ps 51:12, first part

20. Is God willing to do this? 1 John 2:1, 2; Micah 7:18, 19

21. How only did David expect to walk at liberty, or be kept from falling? Ps.51: 12, see 1Cor 3:17, 1Cor 15:57, 58

22. What is the result of the indwelling of the Spirit of God in the hearts of men? Ps. 51:13, Isa 6:7, 8; see John 1:40, 41, 43, 45

23. May we know that God will hear such prayers as David offered? Ps 51:16, 17; Isa 57:15

LESSON 6
May 12, 2018
DELIGHT IN GOD'S HOUSE
PS 84:1-12.
(MEMORY VERSES, 9-12.)

GOLDEN TEXT -" Blessed are they that dwell in Thy house." Ps 84:4.

INTRODUCTION—This psalm is divided into three parts of four verses each, the first four verses referring to God's house, the second to the source of strength, the third is the blessings of God's presence.

1. How did the Psalmist regard the tabernacle of the Lord? Ps 84:1

NOTE —The term "tabernacle" means '"dwelling place of God," and generally applies to the sanctuary in the wilderness, or the temple that succeeded it. As the Presence of God dwelt in the earthly tabernacle, Inspiration uses it as a type of the spiritual house of God.

2. How great was his longing for the house of God? Ps 84:2

3. Why did he long for the courts of God? Last part of Ps 84:2

4. By what example does he illustrate the tender love of God? Ps 51:3

NOTE—Boothroyd gives an altogether different rendering of this verse, which he contends the original justifies, and which considerably changes the meaning: " Yea, as the sparrow findeth a house, and the swallow a nest for herself where she may lay her young, so I seek thine altars, Jehovah, God of hosts, my King and my God." The thought is that just as the sparrow and swallow make it their first business, when the season comes, to build a nest, (a home), so the child of God seeks the altars of God, where he may dwell in the presence of his King. The sense is clearer than is expressed in the common version. If the idea expressed in our text is correct, it would illustrate the peace and safety of the house of God, even to the birds, whose instinct led them there. If instinct, how much more faith.

5. What does the Psalmist say of those who dwell in God's house? Ps 84: 4

NOTE—The Psalmist could not have had reference to living in the literal tabernacle or temple, for this fact of itself does not change the character. For the iniquity committed by those connected with the literal temple see Ezekiel 8, and the case of Eli and sons, 1 Samuel Chapters 2-4. The literal temple of God would be too narrow a meaning. The spiritual house of God, the church, the temple, built by Christ is evidently meant. Zech 6: 13. The word "Selah" occurs some seventy-four times in the. Bible. The rabbis held it to mean "forever," but it is generally considered as indicating some change in the music.

6. In what house of God may we abide and be blessed ? Eph 2:20-22 ; Heb 3: 6

7. How should we regard the assembling together of the people of God? Heb 10:25; John 4: 24

8. What alone makes the meeting-place of God's people precious? Matt 18: 20

9. What does the Psalmist say of those who are strong in the Lord? Ps 84: 5

NOTE.—Boothroyd renders the last part of the verse, "Confidence reigns in the heart." The Revised Version, "In whose heart are the highways of Zion."

10. What does even the desolate land of weeping (Baca, a place of weeping), become to them? Ps 84: 6

> NOTE.—Though they pass through the desolate valley, yet shall they drink from a fountain; yea, the [early, R. V.] rain shall cover it with blessings."—Boothroyd. See Jer 17:8

11. What is this fountain, or well, from which they drink? John 4:13, 14

12. What marks the course of those who thus trust God? Ps 84: 7

13. By what power do they make this progress? Rom 1:16, 17

14. What petition does the Psalmist make for such attainments? Ps 84: 8

> NOTE.—His petition is to the Ever-living One, the God of Hosts, who is abundantly able to help, the covenant God, who cannot break his promise.

15. By what term does he show that he trusts in God? Ps 84: 9, first clause

16. Whom does he present before God in his behalf? Ps 84:9, last clause God's Anointed is the Messiah, our Lord Jesus Christ. See John 1:41, margin

17. What comparison does he make between God's house, the time spent there, and those places and times when God's presence is not manifested? Ps 84:10

18. What does he say that God is to his people? Ps 84:11, first part

NOTE.—The sun gives light, the shield protects. Such is God to his people. He is a light in darkness, he protects in danger. His light leads in duty; his strength or shield defends in the conflict.

19. What will he give to his people? Ps 84:11, second clause

20. Into what will God's grace ripen in the hearts of those who receive it? Rom 5:1, 2; Eph 1:6, 18

21. How are the gifts of God summed up to us? Ps 84:11, last clause (See Rom 8:28)

22. What does the Psalmist conclude in view of God's goodness and power? Ps 84:12

28

LESSON 7
May 19, 2018
A SONG OF PRAISE
Ps 103:1-22
(MEMORY VERSES, Ps 103:1-5)

GOLDEN TEXT-" Bless the Lord, O my soul, and forget not all his benefits."
Ps 103: 2

1. To what extent did David consider the Lord worthy of praise or blessing? Ps 103: 1

2. What duty did he enjoin with the blessing? Ps 103: 2

3. What did he name among these benefits? Ps 103:3-6

4. In forgiving the iniquities of those who receive him, what does God impute and impart to them? Rom 4:6, 7; 3: 22

5. What is a necessary accompaniment of righteousness? Rom 5:18; 8:10, last clause

6. Is healing of disease always accomplished here for those who possess that life? See 2 Tim 4:20; Heb 35-38

7. But, if we go on from faith to faith, of what is that life or spirit within us a pledge? Rom 5:17; 8:11

8. When, then, will all diseases be healed? Rom 8:11; Isa 25:8, 9; 33:24

NOTE.—That Ps. 103:3 is sometimes true in particular cases in this life is abundantly verified; but, with very few exceptions, all of the race have eventually yielded to disease and death. While forgiveness and healing are both classed together, God has declared over and over again that he would forgive all of our sins while we are mortal. This we know to be his will. We may plead it with all confidence. But God has never declared that he would heal all diseases here. In the life hereafter, however, all diseases will be healed; we will be made immortal, incorruptible, like our blessed Lord (Phil. 3:21); of this God has given us a pledge in granting us forgiveness of sin, and bestowing upon us the gift of righteousness, which is also the gift of life—eternal life—as we continue to dwell in Him. John 15:4,5

9. What blessings are scattered on the path of all continually? Ps 103:4; 34:22

10. When will God execute judgment for the oppressed? Ps 103: 6; 50:3, 4

NOTE—Sometimes in this life right is defended—or evil discerned and punished, but none will be passed over in the judgment to come, and every decision will at that time be fair and just and righteous. (John 7:24) Until then, we can know that God will one day bring everything into the light and make all things right.   Note by MD

11. To whom did God reveal his ways for all the children of men? Ps 103:7

12. Among these ways what precious trait of character has he revealed? Ex 34:6, 7; Ps 103:8

13. How will he ever regard the truly penitent, even though his sins have been grievous? Ps 103:9; Micah 7:18

14. What do our sins merit us? Rom 6: 23

15. What proof is given that God has been gracious to us, has dealt with us better than we deserve? Ps 103: 10-12

16. How does he regard our weaknesses? Ps 103: 13, 14; Isa 63:9; Heb. 4:15

17. How is God's mercy compared. with man's frailty? Ps 103:15-18

18. Who beside the obedient may be the recipients of God's mercies? Isa 55:7

19. What reason do we have besides God's wondrous mercy for trusting in him? Ps 103:19; Jude 24

20. Because of all these wondrous manifestations of God's character, how extensive should be the praise offered him? Ps 103: 20-22

21. In view of all God's goodness to us, what should we not forget? Ps 103:2

LESSON 8
May 26, 2018
DANIEL AND HIS COMPANIONS
Dan 1:8-21
(MEMORY VERSES Dan 1:17-19)

GOLDEN TEXT.-" Daniel purposed in his heart that he would not defile himself with the portion of the king's meat, nor with the wine which he drank." Dan 1: 8.

INTRODUCTION.—The time covered by this lesson was 606 to 603 B. C. Jeremiah (25:1) says it was in the fourth year of Jehoiakim; Daniel says (Dan.1: 1), in the third year of the same king. It is supposed that Jeremiah followed the Jewish mode of reckoning, counting a part of an unfinished year the whole year, even though that part consisted of only a few months. Jehoiakim reigned two full years and parts of two other years, counted as years by Jeremiah. Daniel followed the Assyrian mode, which began the reign of any king from the next new year after his accession to the throne. For instance, if a new king's reign should begin in August, the old king's reign would be continued in the chronological accounts till the new year came, and then the reign of the new king would begin. Thus both Jeremiah and Daniel are correct. The place of our lesson was Babylon, a great city, then in the height of its power, 500 miles east of Jerusalem, in the valley of the Euphrates.

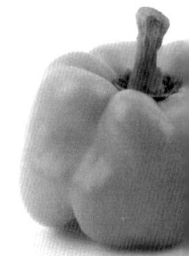

1. Because of the folly of Hezekiah what prediction did the Lord make concerning that king's seed? Isa 39:5-7

2. Who among these did Nebuchadnezzar choose for the purpose of giving them an education in the affairs of state? Dan 1: 3, 4

NOTE.—Mark the character of those chosen. The word " children " is " youths " in the Revised Version.

3. What daily provision was made for their physical needs? Dan 1: 5, first part

NOTE.—The word " meat " simply means "food." This use is quite common in England now. It is used in America in speaking of the kernel of a nut.

4. For how long were they to be thus taught and nourished? Same verse, last part

5. What ones who afterward became noted were among these youths of Israel? Dan 1: 6

6. What change did Ashpenaz make in the names of these young men? Dan 1: 7

NOTE.—Evidently the king designed by this sumptuous fare, the great pains taken with them, and the flattering names given to them, to win them from their own religion to that of Babylon. As their own names brought to their mind the God of Israel, so the names given them connected them with heathen gods. Daniel meant "God is my judge," or "God's judge"; Hananiah, "whom Jehovah graciously gave"; Mishael, " who is what God Is"; Azariah, "whom Jehovah aids." Their names given by Nebuchadnezzar were Belteshazzar, "favored by Bel"; Shadrach, "command of Aku (the moon-god)"; Meshach, Peloubet says, "perhaps connected with Mas, a protecting genius or demigod"; Abed-nego, "servant of Nebo".

7. What course did Daniel and his companions take with reference to the food furnished from the royal table? Dan 1:8.

NOTE—The food furnished Daniel might have been objectionable to him for several reasons: (1) It might have been contrary to the law of God (Leviticus 11); (2) it might not have been properly cleansed from blood (Lev 17: 10); (3) it might have been offered to idols; (4) it might have been rich and unhealthful (Prov 23:1-3). The wine was doubtless intoxicating, and he remembered the words of the Lord through his royal progenitor. Prov 23:29-32

8. By what were they tempted?

NOTE—"They were tempted :
(1) By appetite; the loveof the king's luxuries and wine.
(2) By their ambitions and hopes of success. How could they expect to succeedwith a heathen king, when they were so set in a religion which condemned him and his conduct?
(3) By the king's command. Why should they not yield to it as to an inevitable necessity—their very life might depend upon it.
(4) By the love of prosperity. Their course would make them appear odd, and subject them to ridicule, and bring them into many troubles."—Peloubet. Many Christians professing to be looking for Christ's coming yield principle under much lighter temptations.

9. How had God already begun to work for Daniel? Dan 1:9, see Gen 39: 21 23.

10. What reply did the prince of the eunuchs make? Dan 1: 10.

11. How fairly did Daniel present the matter? Dan 1: 11-13.

NOTE—Pulse, "grain, vegetables, herbs, opposed to flesh and more delicate food."—Gesenius. "Esculent seeds of leguminous plants, such as beans, peas, lentils."—Century Dictionary. The Hebrew word means "seeds."

12. What did God move Melzar (the steward) to decide? Dan 1:14

13. What was the result of the trial? Dan 1:15, 16.

14. How did God regard the integrity and faith of these young men? Dan 1:17, first part

15. What special favors did he show Daniel? Dan 1:17, last part

16. What did the king find in comparing them with the others who had taken this three years' course of training? Dan 1:18, 19

17. What position did he give them because of this? Dan 1:19, last clause. They were made officers and advisers of responsibility. See Gen 41:46

18. How did the king find them as compared with all the wise and great men of his kingdom? Dan 1:20

19. What is said of how long Daniel continued? Dan 1:21

NOTE.—He lived longer than this, but this date is mentioned as the time when God's people were delivered. There are few Old Testament characters more worthy of study and imitation than Daniel,. "greatly beloved" of God. The secret of his life is shown in his faithfulness and integrity in what many would call a small thing, the mere matter of diet. God, however, vindicated his course and left us his example. Daniel knew that sacrifice or compromise of principle was not a small matter; he could not afford it; neither can any Christian.

"Dare to be a Daniel, dare to stand alone,
Dare to have a purpose firm, dare to make it known."

LESSON 9
June 2, 2018
NEBUCHADNEZZAR'S DREAM
Dan 2:31-49
(MEMORY VERSE Dan 2:44)

GOLDEN TEXT —"All things are naked and opened unto the eyes of Him with whom we have to do," Heb 4: 13.

1. By what means did God trouble the mind of Nebuchadnezzar when he was established in his kingdom? Dan 2: 1

2. What success did he have in learning about his dream and its interpretation from his wise men? What was the king's response to their inability to help him? Dan 2:10-12

3. When the news came to Daniel what did he do? Dan 2:14-16

4. Of whom did Daniel seek counsel and what was the result? Dan 2:17-19, 1:17, last clause

5. To whom did Daniel give all the glory? Dan 2: 20-23

6. For what purpose was the dream given? Dan. 2: 28-30

7. Relate the dream. Dan. 2: 31-35

8. What did Daniel interpret the head of gold to mean? Dan 2: 36-38 *babylon*

36

NOTE—This is an unequivocal starting-point. Nebuchadnezzar, not as a single king, but as representing the
Babylonian dynasty, was the " head of gold." This is
shown by another " kingdom," (not king), following. The
word "king" is used as representing kingdom all through
the book of Daniel.

9. What was represented by the breast and arms
of silver? Dan 2: 39, first part; Dan 5: 30, 31; Dan 8: 20

The mᵒᵈians and the Persians

10. What is represented by the belly and thighs
of brass ? Dan 2: 39, last part; Dan 8:21

11. What did he say of the fourth kingdom?
Dan 2: 40; see Dan 7: 7

12. Of what kingdom have we next a record in
the word of God? Luke 2:1. Caesar was an emperor
of Rome

13. What prediction of this power did God give
nearly a thousand years before Daniel's time?
Deut 28:49, 50

14. What was indicated by the mixture of iron
and clay? Dan 2 : 41, first part

NOTE.—It is well to mark that the division of the empire
is not indicated by the toes, as stated by some commentators,
but by the mixture of iron and clay. As the
feet and toes were part of clay and part of iron, so the kingdom
was to be divided.

15. What would be the characteristics of the
kingdom? Dan 2:41, 42

NOTE.—Great strength and great weakness. Strong to resist any other power, as represented by the iron; so weak as never to become united, because of the intermingling of the clay. The iron well represents imperialism, that which seeks to dominate all, the strongest government among men, while clay represents the republican element, weak in cohesive power, tending always to division. These characteristics have been most prominent in European powers.

16. What effort would these divisions make to unite or amalgamate? Dan 2:43

NOTE.—This is generally understood to refer to intermarriages among royal families, in order to unite governments; but all efforts of man are futile. One line of God's word is mightier than all the powers of earth.

17. What did the prophet declare would occur in the last days of this divided kingdom, as represented by the "stone cut out without hands"? Dan 2: 44

18. How will that kingdom be set up and how long will it endure? Verse 44; Ps 2:8, 9; Luke 1:32, 33

19. What did the prophet of God say of the dream and its interpretation? Dan 2:45

20. What did Daniel's revelation bring him and his companions? Dan 2:46, 48, 49

21. But to whom, as the Revealer of secrets, did the great monarch give the glory after all? Dan 2:47

22. What great truths may we learn from this lesson? Dan 2:44; Isa 46:9, 10; Rom 15:4

LESSON 10
June 9, 2018
THE FIERY FURNACE
Dan 3: 13-25
(MEMORY VERSES, Dan 3:16-18.)

GOLDEN TEXT.—"When thou walkest through the fire, thou shalt not be burned; neither shall the flame kindle upon thee." Ps 43:2

INTRODUCTION.— The date of this lesson is not certain, but was probably about 580 B. c., after Nebuchadnezzar had completed his conquest of surrounding nations, as predicted by Jeremiah (27: 2-8). The place was the plain of Dura, about five miles southeast of Babylon. There is a huge mound of brick there at the present time, about seven yards high, which Offert believes to be the base, or pedestal, of the great image.

1. What idolatrous act did Nebuchadnezzar perform when established in his empire? Dan 3:1

He made an Idol Image of Gold

NOTE—The height of this image was ninety feet, its breadth nine feet. The height probably included that of the pedestal, and, covered with gold plates, could be seen a great distance. It was, doubtless, an image of the protecting divinity of Babylon, Bel-Merodach. The word translated "image" means the image of a man.

2. What decree did he make? Dan 3: 2-7

3. What complaint came to the king in reference to this decree? Dan 3: 8-12

NOTE—The Hebrews were accused by the learned Chaldeans. Doubtless they felt envious because the Hebrews were placed above them.

4. What was then done? Dan 3: 13

5. What question did Nebuchadnezzar ask them? Dan 3: 14

NOTE.—Nebuchadnezzar wished to give the Hebrews a fair trial and all the benefit of any doubt. "Is it of purpose," he asked (see margin), "that you did this."

6. What alternative did he set before them? Dan 3: 15

7. What insult did he offer God? Same verse, last part. See similar boasting in Isa 37: 10-13

8. What time to consider their reply did the three men wish? Dan 3:16

NOTE.—"We are not careful," Revised Version, "We have no need." It was a matter of principle, and, as the principle of right was in their heart, they desired no time. They might have taken time and reasoned:

(1) It is only for once, and that will not change our characters;

(2) we will still hold our own religion at heart;

(3) the king, too, ought to be obeyed; God has made him ruler (Jer 27:6-8), and, of course, we ought to be "subject to the higher powers," as God has ordained;

(4) Nebuchadnezzar had befriended them, and, of course they ought not to displease him

(5) their lives were at stake, and they might do as their fathers had done before them;

(6) if they refused to obey, they would die, but if they yielded, they would live, and how much more good they could then do as rulers in that idolatrous nation. These and other vain excuses might have been urged by these faithful men. But they took the only safe way. They neither parleyed with the enemy, nor did they wish time to consider a matter of right or wrong. They could die, but could not yield. Compromise was sin, and right can never compromise with wrong and remain right.

9. What faith in God did they express? Dan 3:17

10. But if it were not God's will to deliver them, what was their choice? Dan 3:18

NOTE.—They had faith to be saved from trial, in trial, by trial, whatever and whichever way God thought best. For him they could stand alone, but God stands with them. When we stand for God, he stands with us.

11. How did their reply affect the king? What did he command? Dan 3:19, 20

12. How was the command executed? Dan 3:21, 23

13. How were the strong men affected who cast them into the furnace? Dan 3:22

14. What revelation was immediately made to the king? Dan 3:24, 25

NOTE.—The better translation of the term rendered "Son of God" is, doubtless, that of the Revised Version, "a son of the gods." Nebuchadnezzar, a heathen, did not know Christ; and yet it was Christ who was with them. They were with him in the right; he was with them in the suffering.

15. What did the king immediately do? Dan 3:26, 27

16. What acknowledgment did Nebuchadnezzar make? Dan 3:28 He acknowledged their honesty, integrity, and righteousness.

17. What decree did he issue? Dan 3:29

NOTE.—Little did these men know what would be the outcome of their simple faith, that it would be the means of having the knowledge of the great God carried throughout that mighty empire in royal decree, by royal heralds. They decided for God irrespective of consequences. God used their simple faith to enlighten the world. It is always thus.

18. What was done with Shadrach, Meshach, and Abed-nego? Dan 3:30

19. What promise of God was exemplified in the case of these men? Ps 43:2

20. By what power were they kept from sinning against God? Ps 17:4; 119:11

21. How will persecutions always result if faithfully borne? Phil 1:12

LESSON 11
June 16, 2018
THE DEN OF LIONS
Dan 6:16-28
(MEMORY VERSES, Dan 6: 19-22)

GOLDEN TEXT.—"No manner of hurt was found upon him, because he believed in his God." Dan 6:23.

1. On account of his fidelity and ability, what important position was Daniel called to fill in his old age? Dan 6:1-3

2. What spirit did this stir up in the other officers and what did they endeavor to do? Dan. 6:4, first part. See Prov 27:4

3. What was the result of their effort? Why? Dan 6:4, last two parts.

4. To what conclusion did their jealousy and envy lead them? Dan 6:5

5. What action did they take to accomplish Daniel's destruction? Dan 6:6-9. Note the flattery to the king

6. What course did Daniel pursue when he heard that the decree was signed? Dan 6:10

7. How did they lead the king to commit himself in the destruction of Daniel? Dan 6:11, 12

8. How did Daniel's enemies present their complaint? How did it affect the king? Dan 6:13, 14

9. By what means was the king compelled to agree to Daniel's destruction? Dan 6: 15

10. How was the law enforced? What was the hope of the king? Dan 6: 16, 17

11. How did the king pass the night? Dan 6: 18

12. What did he say in his lament before the lions' den in the morning? Dan 6: 19, 20

13. What answer was Daniel able to give? Dan 6: 21, 22

14. By what means and power was Daniel kept? Dan 6: 23; Ps. 34: 7

NOTE. —First of all, Daniel was God's servant, he was not, therefore, the servant of men. 1 Cor 7:23. He knew that right was of God and right would win. He knew that to deny his faith in face of the law was to deny God. It would show his enemies that he did not believe that God would help him in time of trouble. Note that he made no display of his faith or lack of faith; he did not defy the unjust law nor show that he despised it; neither did he cringe or compromise; he simply did as he had always done. His purpose to do God's will was not affected in the least by the law. He was living the heavenly life.

"Count me o'er earth's chosen heroes,—they were souls that stood alone
While the men they agonized for hurled the contumelious stone,
Stood serene, and down the future saw the golden beam incline
To the side of perfect justice, mastered by their faith divine,
By one man's plain truth to manhood and to God's supreme design."
—Lowell.

15. By what means and power are the people of God kept from the super abounding evils of the last days? I Peter 1:5

16. How did the lions treat the accusers of Daniel? Dan 6:24

17. What was the result of this experience for Daniel?   Reworded MD
Dan 6:28

18. How did it impact the cause of God?   Reworded MD
Dan 6:25-27

NOTE.—There is no reason to suppose that Daniel expected great results to flow from his simple faith in God apart from his own connection with God. But such are the acts which God uses to advance his kingdom. Most of his people had departed from him and were in captivity. A new empire ruled the world. The world must be enlightened even if God's people would not do it. God so overruled here, as in the case of Daniel's companions, that the head of the government issued a decree which promulgated the name and somewhat of the character of the "name and character" true God to the entire empire. That very proclamation must have given opportunity to many honest hearts to find the true God. We will never realize the fruits of Daniel's faith till we see the redeemed souls in the kingdom of Christ. God makes the wrath of man to praise him.

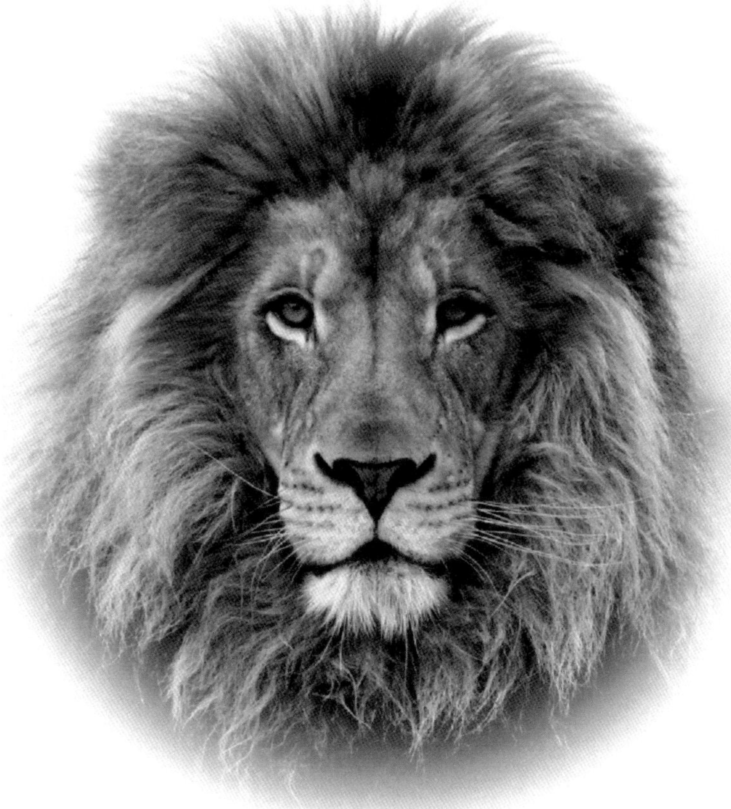

LESSON 12
June 23, 2018
REVIEW

1. In view of Christ's offering, priesthood, and power, what gracious invitation does the Lord extend to the nations of earth? Ps. 2:10-12

2. How does the apostle express the same thing? 2 Cor. 6: 2

3. What is said of the one who trusts Christ?. Ps 2:12

4. What is the character and reward of the one thus blessed? Psalm 1

5. What is the character and reward of the wicked—those who do not trust Christ?

6. How is God revealed through his works? Ps 19:1-6

7. What characteristics of God are revealed in his law? Dan 19: 7-9

8. How should that law be regarded and why? Dan 19:10, 11

9. What should be the continued prayer of every child of God? Dan 19: 12-14

10. Who is able to supply all our needs in these respects? See Psalm 23; John 10:1-16

11. What care does this Shepherd manifest toward his sheep?

12. What is said of his goodness and mercy toward those who trust him?

13. What should be the feelings of every sinner? Ps 51:3-5

14. On what basis alone is God's mercy found? Ps 51: 1

48

5. How much should his prayer embrace?
Ps 51: 7-12

6. What is the result of being cleansed and kept by God?
Ps 51: 13

17. What longings does the Psalmist express concerning God's house?
Psalm 84

18. What does the Lord say of the condition and progress of those who trust in him?

19. What blessings does the Lord pour out upon them?

20. What reasons does the Psalmist give as to why we should praise God?
Psalm 103

21. What lesson of fidelity to conscience and truth have we in the case of Daniel and his companions? and what was its result?

22. Give an account of Nebuchadnezzar's dream.

23. What examples of faith, courage, constancy, and fidelity to God have we in the afterlife of Daniel and his companions ? See lessons 10 and 11

24. Through what do all the blessings brought to view in these lessons, and all the courage and fidelity to God manifested, come?
Heb 11: 6; 1Cor. 1:30, 31

25. Give the golden texts of each lesson.

LESSON 13
June 30, 2018
MESSIAH'S REIGN
PS. 72:1-19
(MEMORY VERSES, Ps. 72:7, 3)

GOLDEN TEXT. —"All kings shall fall down before Him; all nations shall serve Him." Ps. 72:11

INTRODUCTION.—From the title, the introduction, and the close of this psalm, it would seem that it was written by David, a prayer for his son Solomon, who had just ascended the throne, and, through Solomon, predictive of Him, the " Greater than Solomon." The prediction of Christ's reign is colored, or combined, or coalesced, with the royal Psalmist's prayer for his son. The Revised Version gives as an alternative reading of "he shall," and they shall," "let him," "let them," etc., throughout the psalm. This would make it a prayer instead of a prediction. In either case the psalm is true of "great David's Greater Son." Solomon is a twofold type of Christ, or, rather, a type of Christ in two different phases of his work: (1) In building the literal temple of the Lord as Christ builds on his Father's throne the spiritual temple (Zech. 6: 12; 13; Eph. 2:20, 21); (2) in his peaceful reign over the typical promised land after his father had put down all enemies, even as Christ reigns in peace forever in his own kingdom after the Father hath put all foes under his feet (Ps. 110: 1). The work and reign of Christ in both phases are presented in this psalm.

1. What prayer does David make for Solomon? Ps. 72:1

2. Having God's righteousness, how would he judge the people, and what would be their condition? Ps. 72: 2, 3

3. How much more true is this of Christ and his subjects? Ps. 72: 4-7; Isa. 11: 3 and first clause of verse 4

4. How great was the dominion of Solomon? Kings 4:21

5. Over how much of the earth will Christ's kingdom extend? Ps. 72:8

6. What is said of his enemies? Ps.72: 9; Isa.11:4, last part; Rom. 14:11, 12

7. What is said of the homage which shall be rendered to him, and of his character? Ps. 72: 10-14

NOTE.—When this universal homage of Christ is referred to, as it is in several places in the Scriptures, it is not to be understood that all the earth will be converted, and that all kings will yield him willing worship and service. The entire reign of Christ as king, and his great love and pity for his people, manifested throughout the whole of probation, are shown in this psalm. It is true that an unnumbered throng will accept Christ by faith. Rev. 7:9. It is true that when Christ appears, and the wicked dead are raised to be judged, everyone will not only bow before him in the abject and feigned homage of fear and terror (Ps. 66:3, margin; 18:44, margin), but they will also humble themselves before the people of God, whom they have despised (Rev. 3:9). It is true that the wicked will be destroyed root and branch. Mal. 4:-1 ; Obediah 16, and many other places. It is true that all who are then left "will be all righteous," and will with willing hearts serve Christ forever. Isa. 60: 20, 21; Rev. 5:13; 21:24

8. How were these blessings fulfilled in part to King Solomon? 2 Chron. 9:1-9, 20-28.

9. What is further predicted of Christ? Ps. 72: 15.

NOTE.—The Revised Version reads: "And they [those whom Christ saves] shall live; and to him shall be given of the gold of Sheba; and men shall pray for him continually; they shall bless him all the day long." If this be the correct reading, it would seem to have reference to the life which Christ gives through his righteousness to all who trust in him, both here and hereafter. The prayers would be the prayers of saints offered to Christ as High Priest, the prayers perhaps for his coming, and the continual praise which is now offered to him, and will be throughout eternity. If the proper reading is, " He shall live," it would have reference to the eternal triumph of Christ over death. "Knowing that Christ being raised from the dead dieth no more; death bath no more dominion over him." Rom. 6:9; see also Rev. 1: 18 The giving of the gold of Sheba has no doubt some reference to the generous gifts of the people of God in this life, which has been fulfilled in every land and age where the gospel has been preached. It will be preeminently fulfilled in the earth made new. See Rev. 21: 24.

10. What is said of the abundance of Christ's graces and kingdom? Ps. 72:16; Isa. 55: 12, 13

NOTE.—The Revised Version translates Ps. 72:16 as follows: " There shall be abundance of corn in the earth upon the top of the mountains; the fruit thereof shall shake like Lebanon; and they of the city shall flourish like grass of the earth." Boothroyd translates: "Abundance of corn shall be on the ground; on the tops of the mountains its crops shall rustle like the trees that grow on Lebanon; and citizens shall flourish as the grass of the earth." This may denote the abundant blessings of the gospel as well as those of the new earth.

11. What is said of the name of this king? Ps. 72:17, first two clauses; see margin, and Acts 4:12; Jer. 23:6

12. What will come to man through him ? Ps. 72 : 17, last two clauses; Gen. 22: 17, 18

13. Through what do all these blessings come? Gal. 3: 8; Rom. 1:16, 17

14. How far is that gospel to reach? Rev. 14: 6, 7

15. How broad and ample are its provisions? Rom. 10: 12, 13

16. What is said of the condition and blessings of those who bear these glad tidings to the world? Isa. 6: 5-8; Rom. 10: 15

17. How should we feel toward God for the inestimable privilege of being coworkers with him in advancing his kingdom? Ps. 72:18, 19